Collage *and Found Art*

Collage of torn posters found on wall in Rome

Collage of colored and printed papers by Robert Cato

photograph : Milton Glaser

Relief collage of mixed materials by Robert Cato

Children's drawing on Roman wall

photograph : Milton Glaser

COLLAGE *And Found Art*

Dona Meilach
Elvie Ten Hoor

Reinhold Publishing Corporation
New York
an Art Horizons book

To Mel and Perry

Contents

Introduction

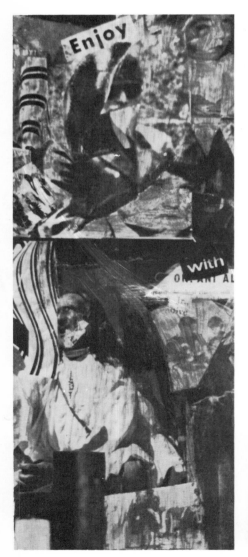

Collage has enormous appeal as an art technique. It provides the artist, young or old, with an amazing range of materials that can be used easily to express his ideas. Unlike oils, watercolors, and most other techniques, collage does not require hours of practice before a satisfactory work of art can be developed. It allows the technical aspects so discouraging to the inexperienced to become secondary to the primary concern of a work of art—content.

Collage also helps develop and reinforce an attitude that proves valuable in all forms of creative expression. Working with collage and found art materials encourages the artist to take a fresh look at the most mundane items. He must learn to divorce them from their everyday functions and give them a new image. Paper, for example, is not limited to being a flat rectangle for writing or wrapping. Crumpled, it is a mass of irregular planes with interacting facets of light and shadow, shallowness and depth. Torn or stripped, it expresses vigorous direction and motion. Wet, it is wispy, fragile. Other everyday materials, including textile scraps, metals, cutouts, and found objects, assume a new character and importance in the hands of the collage artist.

Collage is an excellent means of exploring the principles of composition and design. One of its great advantages is that it permits the artist to arrange and rearrange the compositional elements until he is satisfied with their relationships. He can see the work of art as a whole and evaluate it before it is finished. Are the colors and shapes harmonious? Are the lines and masses integrated and expressive? If so, paste and you have a finished picture. If not, shift, trim, add, subtract, and arrange again.

Anyone with the urge to create will find collage an exciting technique. The collages presented on the following pages were done by children, adult beginners, professional artists, and master artists of the 20th century whose works have entered the stream of art history. Each illustration is a stimulating combination of ideas, experiences, and techniques. They are presented as sources of inspiration and as aids to develop an awareness of the aesthetic potentials inherent in the most commonplace materials and objects.

Dona Meilach
Elvie Ten Hoor

Tools and Materials

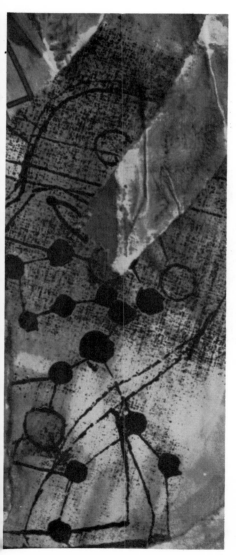

Only a few simple and relatively inexpensive tools and materials are required. Basic materials are listed below, and the sections in the text dealing with specific collage and found art techniques discuss the materials particular to them.

A word of caution about adhesives (glue, paste, etc.) and mounting boards: While most of the materials used in making collages are very inexpensive—or cost nothing at all—adhesives and mounting boards should, whenever possible, be of the best quality. Too many beautifully composed collages have deteriorated simply because the glues and mounts were of inferior quality. A small extra investment in these items will assure greater permanence and allow you greater ease and freedom to express your ideas.

MOUNTING BOARDS

Masonite, sheets of watercolor boards, canvas boards, and stretched canvas are best. For the beginner and for preliminary studies, chipboard and posterboard may also be used. Anything thinner tends to buckle from the moisture of the paste. Construction paper does not make a good backing because when moistened it becomes weak and may tear. Only the heaviest boards should be used for relief collage.

ADHERENTS

The white emulsion glues (Wilhold, Elmer's, etc.) are excellent for collage work. They are durable, easy to use, and transparent when dry. Library paste is good, but it tends to lump and is not as permanent as the emulsion glues. Both emulsion glues and library paste may be thinned with water. Rubber cement should never be used; it fails to make a permanent bond and shows through lightweight papers.

PASTE BRUSHES

A large brush is needed for broad areas. Trying to cover a large space with a small brush is almost impossible, as the initially applied paste will dry before you finish brushing the entire area. Small brushes, of course, are ideal for small paste-ups. Although dime store brushes are adequate, they tend to splay and lose bristles. Inexpensive oil painting bristle brushes are excellent.

CUTTING MATERIALS

Scissors are needed for forming large areas and cutting small details. Rulers and other straight edges are good aids for tearing. Single-edge razor blades and mat knives are useful for cutting already attached papers and shaping details.

OTHER MATERIALS

Sponges are handy for removing excess paste and water and for making corrections (see Technical Notes, p. 68). Large plastic bowls come in handy when wetting paper and washing up. Water-filled jars or cans should be available for cleaning brushes. (Glue should never be allowed to dry on brushes; it ruins them.) Tweezers are helpful in handling bits and details. Last, but hardly least, is the working area. To avoid the tiresome task of scraping up dried glue and repairing nicks and scratches on good table tops, use easily washed heavy coverings like oilcloth or plastic, or a vinyl or formica covered working board.

1
Torn and Cut Paper Collages

Paper is the classic material for collage. Its versatility is amazing. Paper can be torn, cut, shredded, crumpled, and it adheres readily to most surfaces.

This chapter deals mostly with plain, unprinted papers, as they encourage the artist to develop an awareness of line, shape and color contrast before going on to the more complicated techniques. Unprinted papers are available in a wide range of weights, textures and colors—both opaque and semi-transparent.

Construction paper in particular offers a large assortment of colors, both bright and subdued. Butcher paper and newsprint are dull in color, but they are very inexpensive and act as subtle contrasts to brighter, textured papers. These papers can, of course, be painted with watercolor or poster paints in any color desired. Blotting paper is available in a limited range of colors and provides textural contrast to the thinner papers.

One of the most rewarding papers for collage is art tissue. It is sold in a variety of rich colors and is semi-transparent. This latter quality permits the artist to develop many interesting color and value effects by overlapping the tissues.

To this list one could add unusual materials, such as cellophane, waxed paper, paper bags, and any other common, solid-color papers.

1. A classroom art assignment was given that concentrated on developing simple designs. The materials are black, gray, and white construction paper. The geometric shapes alone produce interest, setting up tension and movement. The background is designed as an important part of the composition.

2. The forms in this construction paper collage are symmetrically balanced.

1. *DESIGN IN WHITE, BLACK, AND GRAY by Carol Rufini, 5th grade*

Although the shapes are quite flat, the strong value contrast creates a feeling of depth. Children are frequently better able to develop good design when working with abstract shapes rather than with realistic images.

3. The butterfly was formed from small, irregularly cut bits of colored paper. The spaces between the pasted bits are varied in size and shape, indicating a strong awareness of the role of negative spaces in design.

2. BLACK AND GRAY ON WHITE
by Guy Mazza, 5th grade

3. BUTTERFLY by 2nd grade student

4. This is a study for the crowning achievement of Matisse's later years— the stained glass windows for the Chapel of the Rosary at Vence, France. The shapes were cut from papers colored with gouache.

5. The clown is exuberantly executed in torn construction paper. Young children tend to concentrate only on the central figure, without considering the picture as a whole. Encouraging them to construct backgrounds with torn shapes makes them aware that backgrounds are also important.

6. Torn paper strips create a dynamic abstraction of a Shinto shrine. The design suggests Oriental calligraphy. Heavy colored papers and paper bags were used. To keep the papers from deteriorating, Liquitex polymer medium was brushed over the finished work.

4. *MAQUETTE FOR NUIT DE NOEL by Henri Matisse, 1952. Collection: Museum of Modern Art, New York. Gift of Time, Inc.*

5. *CLOWN by Nancy Scofield, pre-school*

6. *SHINTO SHRINE by Ann Roman, 1962*

7. *LIGHTS OF THE CITY by Dona Meilach*

8. *STILL LIFE by Elvie Ten Hoor*

9. *GERANIUMS by Elvie Ten Hoor*

10. *AUTUMN by Elvie Ten Hoor*

7. Abstraction of a small city and surrounding farmlands as viewed at night from an airplane. The larger shapes of the tilled and planted acres enclose the city, whose lighted main streets are represented by the small, bright rectangles. The materials are construction paper, Oriental paper, and tissue.

8. These flowers were formed from one of the most versatile collage materials: art tissue. Because the tissue is semi-transparent, variations in value and color can be created by overlapping.

9. Art tissue lends itself to any stylistic approach, realistic or abstract. In this collage, the subject is interpreted abstractly, emphasizing shapes and values. The dark and light accents were cut from red and black tissues and heavier papers. "Cutting and pasting is much neater and easier than painting," said the artist. "If a shadow didn't look quite right, I moved the paper or changed the shape and tone until it was right. Then I pasted it."

10. This abstraction of a sun-spattered forest floor is given a feeling of depth by placing large torn shapes below and increasingly smaller ones toward the top. The torn tissue and Oriental papers are in autumn colors—reds, yellows, rusts, browns, and blues. A landscape like this may be designed from photographs.

11. *CAT UP A TREE by Dennise Stokes, age 13*

12. *RINGMASTER (after Toulouse-Lautrec) by Elvie Ten Hoor*

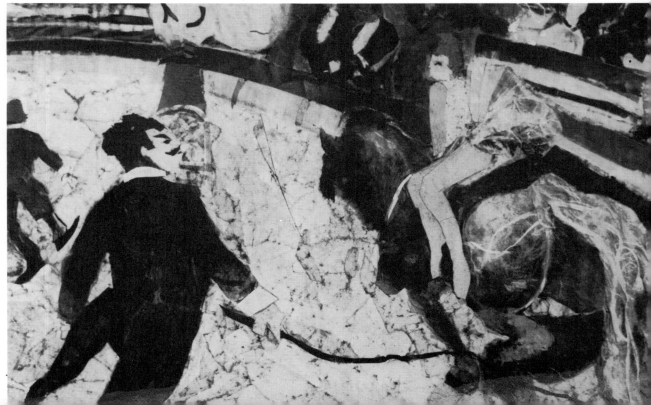

13. *CONGO GIRL by Nancy Wasserman, 12th grade*

14. *PORTRAIT IN PAPER by Rita Spaulding, 1961*

11. The spontaneity of tearing papers encourages fresh, bright interpretation. In this instance, a cat with an impertinent expression was developed with torn art tissue. The mood is light, yet obviously the technical aspects of good composition were seriously considered.

12. A famous oil painting has been sensitively recreated as a torn tissue and textured paper collage. Although the subject is recognizable and accurate in placement and feeling to the original, this collage is a creative impression rather than a copy. For those who find design difficult, interpreting a favorite painting through collage can be instructive and enjoyable. Analyzing shapes, lines, colors, and movement promotes greater awareness of their relationships in good design.

13. Watercolored manila paper was cut and pasted to form the head; construction paper was used for the hands. The picture does not attempt to portray; it is a design of the features, tattoos and painted tribal marks of an imaginary young African.

14. This is an attempt to create the mood, features, and character of an individual. The subject's face was analyzed as a three-dimensional form: protruding nose, inset eyes, high cheekbones, strong chin. The irregularly cut and torn tissue paper pieces were laid one over the other to build up these relationships.

15. *SOUTHERN SPLENDOR by Oril Sorby*

15. An unusual characteristic of Oriental papers is the fact that they are held together by strands of straw or silk. This gives them strength as well as texture. In this example, taiten paper, a very fine paper with delicate texture, was used to create the spidery effect of the foliage by the following method: First, the composition was sketched on the backing board. Then a piece of tissue in a color basic to the entire color scheme was glued to the board. Since tissue is semi-transparent, the sketch showed through. Background areas and the tree trunks were formed with tissue and heavy papers. To make the foliage, large pieces of taiten paper were brushed with white emulsion glue thinned with water, and quickly placed on the board. They were shaped with a brush and the fingers. When the paper was dry, it had almost disappeared into the background, leaving the fibers exposed.

16. Art tissue may be modeled, shaped, pulled, and wrinkled when it is thoroughly moistened with emulsion blue and water. This sequence illustrates some of the ways to model tissue paper. The steps can be applied to most sculptured tissue collages: (1) Tear a piece of tissue larger than the finished shape you have in mind. This will allow plenty of material to model with, without reducing the desired size of the shape. (2) Moisten the tissue with watery emulsion glue until it is soft and pliable. (3) Place it on the board, and model. It can be bunched, pulled, and squeezed for a variety of effects. But work gently; wet tissue is very fragile. To create the owls' texture, the artist pulled gently downward on the bodies and pushed the paper together to form feathery wings.

17. This simple, graphic design delicately balances torn tissue shapes with open spaces. Thin ruled lines and printed papers are used for accents.

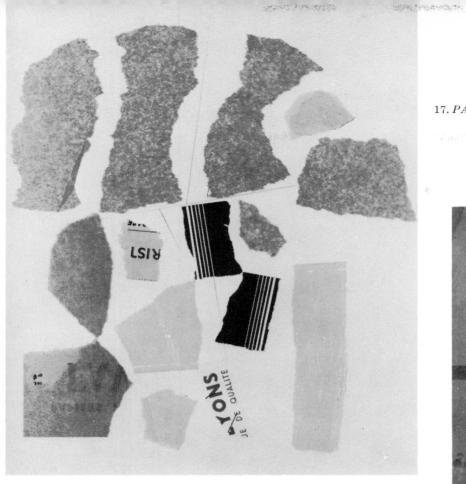

16. *THE OWLS by Elvie Ten Hoor*

2
Jig-Saw Collages

Making a collage from patterned and
printed papers is rather like assembling
the jumbled pieces of a jig-saw puzzle
into a picture. However, in the jig-saw
puzzle the picture is built into the separate
pieces, while in the collage the picture
is in the mind of the artist. The collage,
therefore, requires far greater ingenuity.
An ambitious collage may involve
numerous attempts at arrangement,
ideas being modified or discarded along
the way until a satisfying design has
been worked out.

Unlike the jig-saw puzzle pieces, the
collage elements must be provided by the
artist. This poses no problem at all.
No other material for fashioning works
of art is so abundant and easily obtained.
The range of materials is suggested by
the collages reproduced in this chapter.
They include almost anything printed or
patterned. Their use is equally wide:
the pieces may become shapes, produce
lines, or provide color and texture to
build the image in mind.

PATTERNED PAPERS

There are, quite literally, several
hundred kinds of patterned papers, from
artistically designed ones to everyday
throw-aways. The former include
wallpapers, bookbinder's end papers,

18. *VISITING THE STATUE OF
LIBERTY by Elyse Garland, age 12*

decorative wrapping papers, and over 300 kinds of machine and handmade imported papers. (For a partial list of Oriental papers, see Technical Notes, p. 68). The throw-aways include the daily newspaper, catalogs, theatre handbills, ticket stubs, and things you probably have right now in your pocket.

18. The shapes in this delightful collage, a recollection of a vacation trip to the Statue of Liberty, were cut from colored construction paper and magazine pictures. The few patterned paper accents were cut from magazine illustrations. Fashion magazines, in particular, offer a wonderful and cheap source of patterned papers.

19. The exuberant boy chasing his kite reflects the mood of the young artist, who chose the cutouts from patterned papers and magazines. Please note the tree—french-fried potatoes.

19. *KITE FLYER by Susan Meilach,*
7th grade

20. *MODERN JAPANESE COLLAGE by Aiko Nakane*

21. *COLLAGE WALL PANEL by Caroline Duer, c. 1900. Courtesy:
The Cooper Union Museum, New York*

20. Oriental papers provide an almost inexhaustible source of beautiful patterns. This collage is a modern interpretation of an ancient Japanese art—setting calligraphy on highly decorative backgrounds.

21. The Victorian housewife occupied her spare time with various forms of busywork—some now acclaimed as folk art. Among her diversions was separating large machine-printed sheets of flowers, leaves, birds, angels, etc., and recombining them to make something decorative— in this case a wall panel.

22. Fancy end papers, which are employed in custom bookbinding, are used here to make a magazine illustration. The marbelized papers bear a curious resemblance to a telescopic view of planets, illustrating that patterned papers may be found to suit almost any need. The rocket is made of torn tissue.

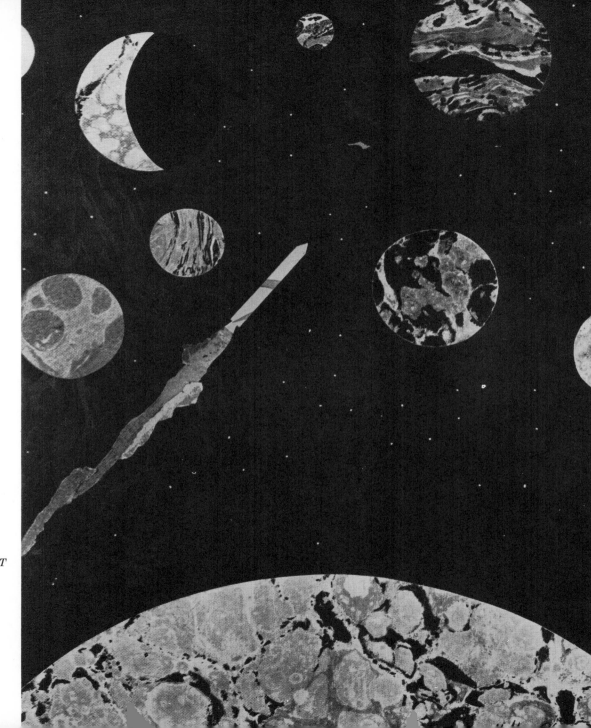

22. *SPACE SHOT*
by Milton Glaser

23. Another use of collage as illustration. In this interesting approach, the head of Chopin is defined as a negative image by building up a background of torn, richly patterned papers.

24. Kurt Schwitters is one of the master collage makers of the 20th century. He turned to collage because he felt that oil on canvas was too confining. He said, "When I adjust materials of different kinds to one another, I have taken a step in advance of mere oil painting, for in addition to playing off color against color, line against line, and form against form, I play off material against material. . . ."

Everybody's Favorite Series No. 56

&

Amsco Music Publishing Company $1.75

Chopin Album

Contents:
Ballade, Op. 23
Ballade, Op. 47
Berceuse, Op. 57
Etude, Op. 10, No. 3
Revolutionary Etude, Op. 10, No. 12
Fantasie Impromptu
Impromptu, Op. 29
Marche Funebre, Op. 35
Mazurka, Op. 7, No. 1

Mazurka, Op. 17, No. 1
Mazurka, Op. 24, No. 3
Mazurka, Op. 68, No. 2
Mazurka, Op. 68, No. 3
Nocturne, Op. 9, No. 2
Nocturne, Op. 27, No. 2
Nocturne, Op. 37, No. 1
Nocturne, Op. 37, No. 2
Nocturne, Op. 48, No. 1
Polonaise, Op. 26, No. 1

Polonaise in A, Op. 40, No. 1 (Military)
Polonaise, Op. 40, No. 2
Polonaise, Op. 53 Ab
Prelude, Op. 28, No. 4
Prelude, Op. 28, No. 6
Prelude, Op. 28, No. 7
Prelude, Op. 28, No. 15
Prelude, Op. 28, No. 24
Valse in E Minor

Valse Brillante,
Valse, Op. 42
Valse, Op. 64, No.
(Minute Wa
Valse, Op. 64, No.
Valse, Op. 69, N
Valse, Op. 69, N
Valse, Op. 70, N
SAMUEL SPIVAK
Editor

23. *CHOPIN* by Isadore Seltzer

24. *AUFRUF by Kurt Schwitters, 1919.*
Courtesy: The Art Institute of
Chicago, gift of Mr. and Mrs. Maurice
E. Culberg

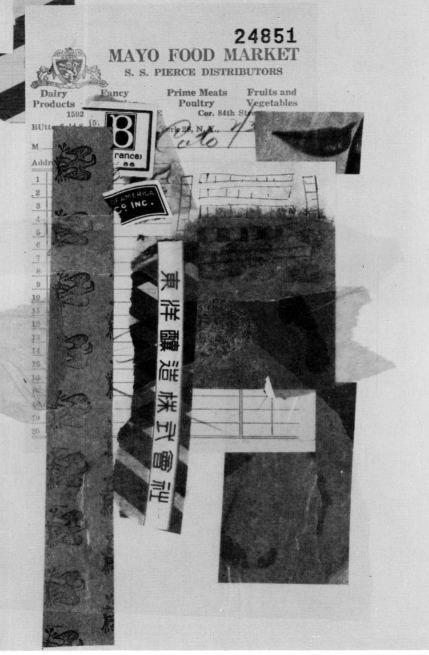

25. Commonplace printed materials, including a bill from the local market, are enhanced by overlays of torn and cut semi-transparent papers. The result creates a surprisingly three dimensional feeling.

26. Antique bank notes, some yellowed with age, have been grouped with newspaper and hand-colored bond paper. The precisely arranged result is enlivened by a swath of torn black paper pieces.

25. *24851 by Robert Cato*

26. *BANKNOTES by Ralph Arnold, 1961*

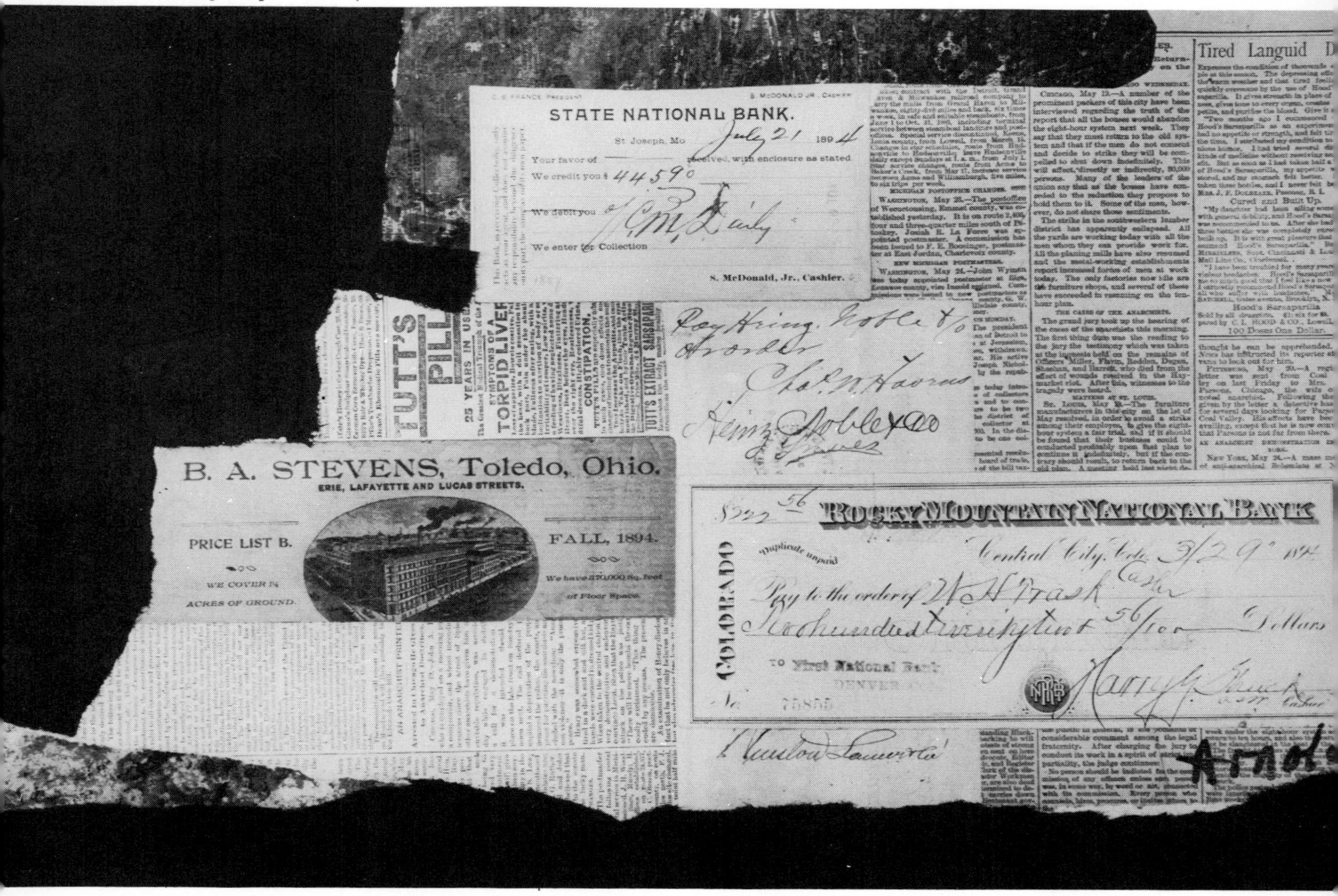

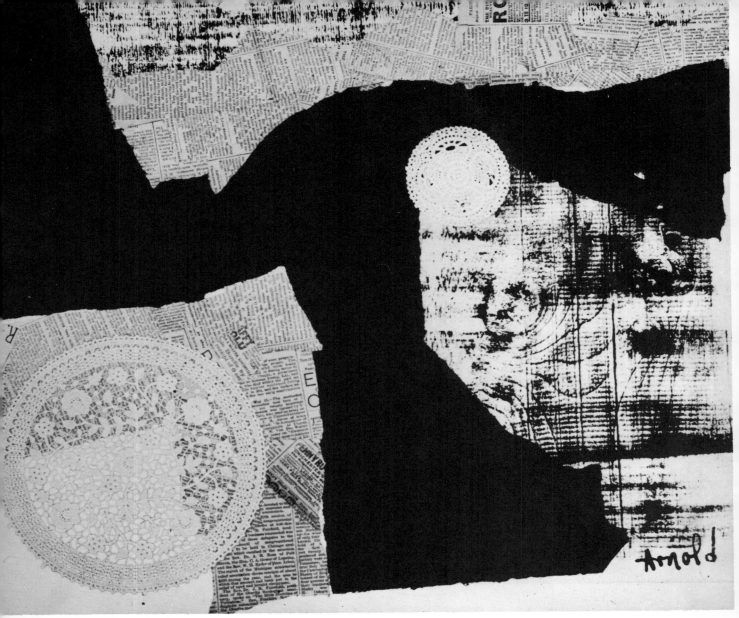

27. *BLACK AND WHITE ANTIQUE* by Ralph Arnold, 1962

27. A bold black form emerges from
shapes composed of torn newspaper and
paper doilies. The wood-grained
background is patterned Oriental paper.

GALA DAY AT ST. CROIX by Elvie Ten Hoor. Torn and cut Oriental papers

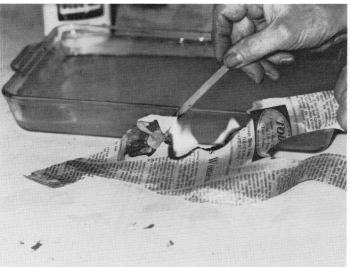

28. *SPRING by Ralph Arnold*

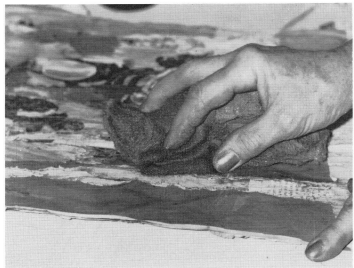

28. Paper may be treated in a number of interesting ways before it is applied. These pictures illustrate burning an interesting shape, glueing it down, then lightly rubbing it with very fine steel wool to remove the carbonized bits.

29. In addition to charring paper, the artist has used another interesting method. He built up several layers of newspaper and charred paper. Then he dug into the top layers and tore them off to reveal the lower layers. The edges were smoothed with steel wool. The result resembles the jagged mountains and rock formations of the Southwest.

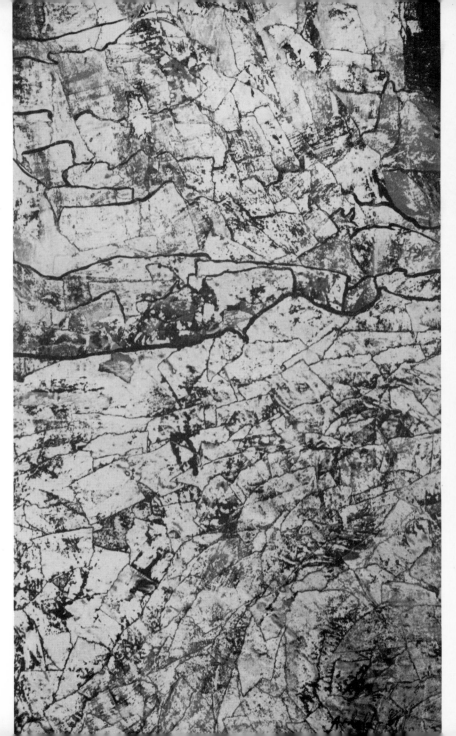

29. *CLIFF IMAGES by Ralph Arnold, 1961*

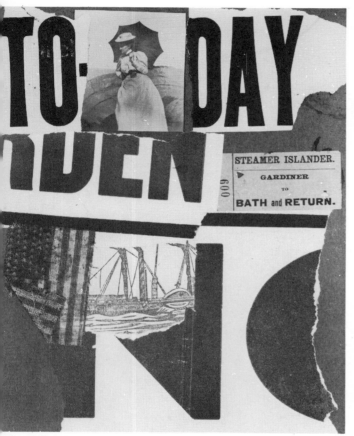

30. *BATH AND RETURN by Robert Weaver*

31. *MOTHER ALWAYS TOLD ME*
by Gabriel Morera, 1963

FIGURATIVE CUTOUTS

One of the most popular and amusing sources of collage materials is the magazine. Any illustrated magazine will do: news, trade journal, movie star, comic, home decorating, or fashion. Frequently only a single copy will provide enough material for several collages.

There may be one obstacle to working with magazine photographs and illustrations—they are already complete artistic interpretations. The photographer composed his picture, and the illustrator his drawing or painting. For this reason, it is sometimes difficult to divorce the magazine cutout from its original context. To overcome this difficulty, analyze the illustration or photograph as areas of dark and light, texture and color. If it contains figures, they can be cut out and recombined in surprising ways.

30. A nostalgic evocation of a turn-of-the-century holiday uses a variety of mementos from the period, including torn posters, prints, a photograph and a small flag.

31. The figures in this collage were cut from magazines of a half century ago and mounted on stained wrapping papers rescued from the waste basket.

32. A beautifully designed collage, this is also a historical document. The august assembly includes some of the leading artists of the 20th century—among them, Salvador Dali, Man Ray, and Marcel Duchamp.

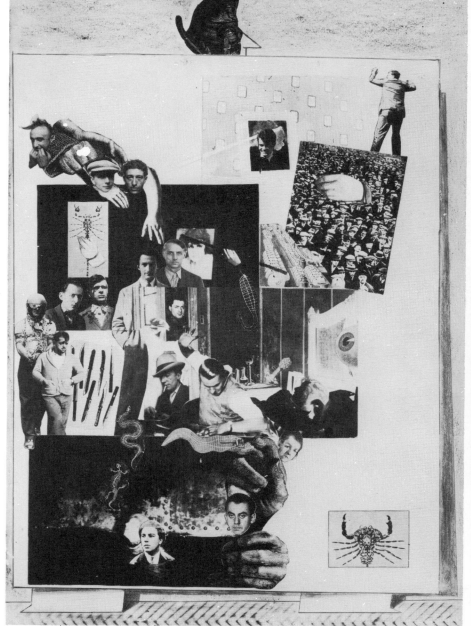

32. *MEMBERS OF THE SURREALIST GROUP by Max Ernst.*
Collection: Museum of Modern Art, New York

33. *MADISON SQUARE GARDEN* by Robert Cato

34. *TRADE MARK* by Robert Cato

33. This lively torn paper collage using ice hockey as a theme employs elements from photographs and the daily newspaper.

34. A sensitive study in value contrasts. The fragmented images of Picasso's dancers, cut from art prints, are combined with printed papers, letters, and a rather ominous photograph.

35. This handsome collage was part of an advertising campaign to motivate travel to Europe. The individual parts include familiar postcard views, stamps, tickets, a Tarot card, old engravings, and famous works of work.

Why do well-traveled people travel Sabena? "Flight-seeing" via helicopter is only part of it. People who know Europe know Sabena shows it off best: with the world's only 3-speed fleet of "Intercontinental" Boeing jets. *Caravelle "Continental" jets and Sikorsky helicopters: with a special savoir-faire that extends to and through Europe, Africa and the Middle East. Next trip ... fly Sabena. Le service Belgique—c'est magnifique!

*(soon)
Ask your Travel Agent to book you Sabena all the way... or simply call Sabena Belgian World Airlines. More than 200 offices in the principal cities of the world

36. *MONTE CARLO SHARE by Marcel Duchamp, 1924. Collection: Museum of Modern Art, New York, gift of the artist*

36. The bitter disillusionment following World War I gave rise to the Dadaists, a group who reasoned that since a world in turmoil was without meaning, art should likewise be meaningless. In revolt they created an "anti-art" using non-art materials. Their irreverent wit and unorthodox designs stimulated later artists to produce serious works using common objects and throw-away materials. In this example the artist has pasted a photograph of himself on a lottery ticket.

37. A photograph of the streamlined typewriter is combined with type and geometric shapes to suggest the interdependence of man and machines in modern industry. The clean-cut designs of Paul Rand established a new trend in advertising.

38. A photomontage effect was developed with magazine cutouts and art prints pasted against an abstract background of torn colored papers.

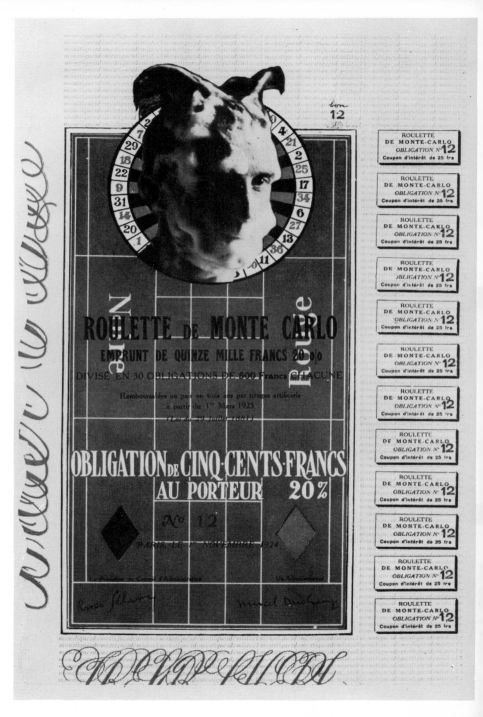

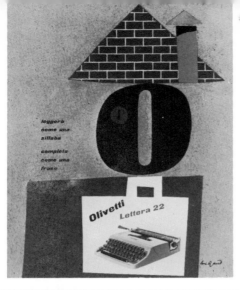

37. *DESIGN FOR OLIVETTI* by Paul Rand

38. *OLD CURIO SHOP* by Elvie Ten Hoor

39. *MASQUERADE by Nancy Carlson, age 11*

39. This ambitious collage took several
months to complete. All the photographs
were cut from *Life* magazine. They
are arranged so that the picture may be
hung in any direction.

3
Textile Collages

Working with textiles involves the same basic considerations as working with papers: choosing the materials, combining them creatively, and pasting them down. Textiles come in an enormous range of patterns, textures and colors. Among the more delicate are silks, nylons, sheer cottons and rayons. Among the more rough and sturdy are wools, corduroys, terrycloths and burlaps. Any of these fabrics, and others too numerous to mention, may be glued together, sewn, or painted.

Textiles require a little more skill and patience in handling than do papers. Heavier textiles are more absorbent than paper and will need more glue. Consequently the pieces will take longer to dry and may slip out of position. A few well-placed straight pins will secure the material until the glue dries. Do not use tape or your fingers to hold the textile in position.

Many fabrics tend to stretch or shred. Allow for stretching when estimating the desired size and shape of the material. Shredding may be avoided by using sharp scissors and by not handling the cut edges unless absolutely necessary. However, from a collage viewpoint, many of the most interesting textiles are those that do shred. If you have a shredded edge you wish to incorporate into your design, you may avoid pasting down each strand by applying glue directly to the backing board and pressing the shredded edges onto it—the easiest method, in fact, for adhering nearly all fabric pieces.

40. Children like working with yarns and fabrics; the materials feel good and can be bent and folded innumerable times without ruining them. This collage was made from yarn, glitter, and fabric scraps and glued on burlap backing.

40. *ANGEL by Marian McCoy, age 11*

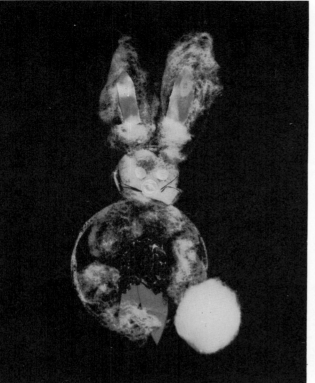

41. *BUNNY by Christine Gannon, age 6*

41. Cotton—a "pre-fabric," one might say—is popular with young children. Animals are also popular and make good collage subject matter. *Bunny* is composed of cotton body, ribbon inner ears, paper torso, button nose and grass whiskers. Learning to relate broad similarities, like the resemblance between a button and a rabbit's nose, is good basic experience in developing the imagination.

42. This homemade fashion plate is a charming example of folk art. The dress and apron materials are all handspun. The collage may have been fashioned from scraps left over from sewing an actual dress and apron.

42. *A COUNTRY WIFE OF WALLACH*
Germanic Folk Art, c. 1820. Courtesy:
The Cooper Union Museum, New York

43. SAXON VILLAGER IN SUNDAY CLOTHES *Germanic Folk Art, c. 1820 Courtesy: The Cooper Union Museum, New York*

44. MR. ELSGOOD AS QUICKSAND *English, 1839. Courtesy: The Cooper Union Museum, New York*

43. The folk artist who made this collage, probably as a companion piece to *Country Wife,* used homespun materials for the pants and coat, chamois for the jacket, and leather for the boots. All were pasted on heavy vellum.

44. In the early 19th century, pasting fabrics, tinsel, embossed foil, and ribbons on a cheap engraving was a popular pastime. One selected a favorite actor from a dealer in theatrical portraits, took him home, and proceeded to dress him according to one's taste, which was sometimes quite splendid—even if a bit flashy.

45. *MR. C. KEMBLE AS PRINCE OF*
   WALES signed W. West, Dec. 1821
   Courtesy: The Cooper Union Museum,
   New York

46. *ABSTRACT STILL LIFE by Elvie Ten Hoor*

45. Mr. Kemble probably made a more elegant Prince of Wales than did the prince himself. Although this and the previous example are not exactly the acme of modern taste, they do indicate that quite a variety of shapes and textures can be made with pasted fabrics.

46. Shredding fabrics provides an interesting means of creating surface texture and pattern. Burlap was used for this flowing design. To shred a fabric, gently pull threads away from the center. Apply glue to the mounting board and press the fabric into it.

47. A self-portrait using paper and fabric. The artist, an illustrator, has placed himself in a sea of magazine covers, the symbols of his profession. The small American flag, worn with age, adds a patriotic design element to this handsome collage.

47. *SELF PORTRAIT* by Robert Weaver

48. *COLLAGE by Ann Ryan, 1953.
Collection: Museum of Modern Art,
New York, given anonymously*

49. *NUMBER 180: AGE OF
COMMUNICATION by Charmion von
Wiegand, 1956. Collection: Museum of
Modern Art, New York, given
anonymously*

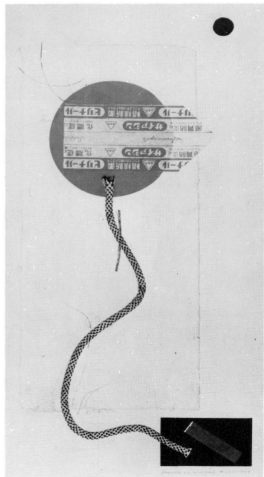

50. *ST. JOHN ON PATMOS by unknown German artist, c. 1750. Courtesy: The Cooper Union Museum, New York*

48. Dark and light rectangles are enclosed by a watercolor paper mat and mounted on linen. The rectangles are cut from printed and textured cotton and other fabrics, colored paper and burlap. The frayed burlap edges enliven the surface texture.

49. The stark simplicity of this non-objective collage relies on tension between rectangles and circles of dark and light. A fabric cord creates rhythm and adds textural variety to the printed and colored papers.

50. Each shape was cut from a colorful printed or textured handmade fabric. The shapes were first roughly glued in place and then stitched, employing the appliqué technique. The lines between the shapes and the tiny details are also stitched.

51. This highly detailed work took months to complete. Many of the smaller elements are no larger than one-eighth inch. The colors are warm, rich shades of rose, green, yellow, tan and blue. The stitching is white and black.

51. *CHRIST CARRYING THE CROSS by unknown German artist, c. 1750. Courtesy: The Cooper Union Museum, New York*

52. *THE OLD PIANO by Elvie Ten Hoor*

52. Anything is potential collage material. Although leather is not a textile, it can be treated as one when used in a collage. Its smooth, naturally lustrous quality is used here in an abstract design. Experimental patterns may be marked on the leather with a piece of chalk, which dusts off easily. If you make a mistake in cutting, don't throw the pieces away. They can be extended with scraps to build up new patterns. To keep the cut shapes from slipping out of place as they are arranged, secure them with thumb tacks.

4
Mixed Media

The previous sections indicate the wide variety of materials that can be combined in a single collage to produce an infinite range of effects.

Now consider the numerous drawing and painting media that can be combined with these materials: pencil, pen and ink, monoprint, charcoal, pastels, gouache, crayon, watercolors, poster paints, and oils, to name a few. In the following collages these media are used to link elements, provide a background for them, accent them, contrast with them, or all of these. They may comprise only a small part of the composition, accenting the major areas constructed in collage materials, or provide the major design elements.

53. A lively collage salute to the Republic. Washington and Lincoln embrace in a sky filled with American eagles cut from paper prints. The flags are fabric. Scribbled pencil lines add an uninhibited note to the composition.

53. *SEMPER FIDELIS by Robert Weaver*

46

54. *MAN WITH A HAT by Pablo Picasso,*
1912. Collection: Museum of Modern
Art, New York

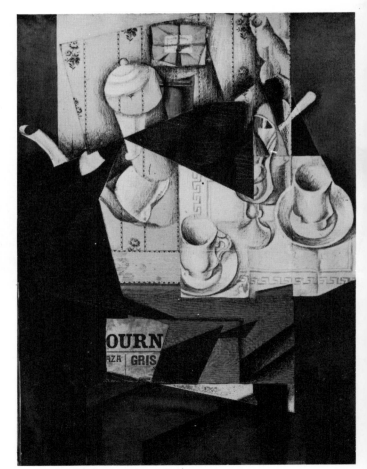

55. *BREAKFAST by Juan Gris, 1914.*
Collection: Museum of Modern Art,
New York, Lillie P. Bliss Bequest

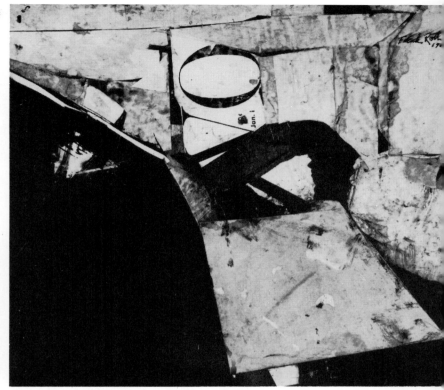

56. *COLLAGE by Corrado di Marca-Relli, 1954. Courtesy: The Art Institute of Chicago, Mr. and Mrs. Frank G. Logan Purchase Prize*

57. *ABSTRACTION by Frank Roth, 1962*

54. Pablo Picasso's unbridled inventiveness has led him to experiment with an unending assortment of materials. Among them are paper, wood, cardboard, tin, bronze, sand, as well as many materials normally foreign to the artist. In this Cubist collage, the materials are charcoal, ink and pasted papers. The two-dimensional surface is maintained by reducing objects to their simplest geometric volumes and planes.

55. Painted paper, crayon, and oil on canvas. While Braque and Picasso seldom used more than a single dull color in their early collages, Gris often combined several colors for a gayer effect. Here, brown, white, and pink paper and paint are arranged against a lively blue background. The collage is a characteristic Cubist work—sharp, geometric, and fragmented.

56. Here the traditional subject of a seated human figure is developed with angular abstract shapes cut from canvas. The shapes were coated on the back with black oil paint; then they were pressed onto a stretched canvas, forcing the paint out around the edges to form irregular linear patterns.

57. Black oil paint is combined with cut and torn papers from *Vogue* magazine. The surface texture is heightened by a semi-transparent varnish glaze.

48

58. *TERRES NOIRES by Jean Dubuffet.
Collection: Museum of Modern Art,
New York, gift of Mr. and Mrs.
Donald H. Peters*

58. Jean Dubuffet is a master of the art
of collage. Many of his most beautiful
paintings are in reality collages made up
of a mosaic of richly painted canvas
pieces glued to heavy canvas support.
Here he has used the simpler technique
of cutting figures from hand-painted
papers.

59. Shapes cut from bond paper were
[glu]ed to a canvas backing. Oil glazes were
[br]ushed onto the surface to heighten
[the] textural effect. The result is a design
[of] great internal movement. The darker
[ar]eas cause the light shapes to burst
[fo]rward, producing a feeling of depth.

59. *UNTITLED NO. 1 by Ronald Ahlstrom.*
(Photograph, Mickey Pallas)

60. *MONOPRINT COLLE* by Elvie Ten Hoor

61. *BOOK JACKET* by Milton Glaser

60. A combination monoprint and collage. To make a monoprint, paint or roll printer's ink or paints onto a sheet of glass; then, while the ink or paint is still wet, lay a sheet of good quality paper over it. Develop a design or pattern by pressing the paper against the inked glass plate with the fingers or a pointed tool. When the design has been pressed in, lift the paper and allow it to dry. Then apply the collage materials.

61. This striking book jacket combines illustration with collage. The flowers were cut from a commercial seed catalog. The background is decorative end paper.

62. A collage spoof of male fashion by one of the leaders of the Dada movement. Hats cut from a clothes catalog are glued to a mounting and embellished with pencil, ink, and watercolor.

63. Ernst was one of the first collage artists to incorporate prints in his work. In this example, printed illustrations have been cut apart and reassembled to produce a handsome—and highly irrational—figurative design. Pencil and ink lines have been added.

62. *THE HAT MAKES THE MAN by Max Ernst. Collection: Museum of Modern Art, New York*

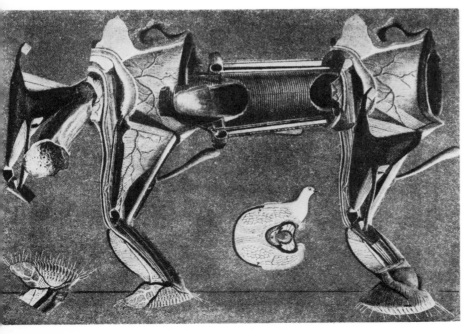

63. *THE HORSE, HE'S SICK by Max Ernst. Collection: Museum of Modern Art, New York*

64. *INTERNAL ARRANGEMENT No. 4*
by Robert W. Anderson, 1962

64. Materials from unusual sources can be given a new meaning by the collage artist. Here, instructive anatomical studies have been divorced from their original use to create an exciting work of art. Pencil and ink lines were added to the pasted figures.

65. A whimsical parody of a favorite classical theme: the idyllic mythological allegory. The protagonists were cut from art prints and the bemused modern spectators (upper right) from a news magazine. Casein, graphite, and pastels were used to blend the figures and mellow the classic seriousness of the scene.

66. This collage is both representational and symbolic. Printing materials— mats, linotype, and newsprint—form a heavily textured background for the figure of a printer, painted in oil. The backing is stretched canvas.

67. Semi-transparent and opaque papers and oil paint express the strength and grandeur of mountain forms. The contrast between the darkest shapes and the light areas gives the impression of depth and space without using perspective.

68. A richly textured collage using a variety of semi-transparent and opaque plain and printed papers combined with casein and shellac. The support is a Masonite panel.

65. *JUDGMENT OF PARIS WITH THE ASSISTANCE OF RUBENS by Robert W. Anderson*

66. *NEWS OF THE DAY by Bruno Caruso, 1962.*
Courtesy: Findley Galleries, Chicago

67. *DAVOS II by Harry Bouras, 1962*

68. *EXCAVATION by Rosamond Berg*

5
Relief Collages

Collage is, by nature, a relief technique. Paper and other materials are pasted one over the other to form a design which is composed of integrated planes. The planes, however, may be so shallowly contrasted that the surface appears to be absolutely flat. The sculptural aspect of collage should be emphasized, for it promotes greater awareness of the beauty that can be developed through structural contrast.

Briefly, there are two major methods for developing structural relief. The first is to build up the picture plane itself. The second is to apply three-dimensional objects to the plane.

BUILT-UP RELIEF

Many interesting relief effects can be developed on the picture plane before applying papers, textiles, and other objects. These effects may cover the entire board or be confined to only a few areas. Building up small isolated areas will produce dynamic effects.

Several modeling materials may be used to build up textures and patterns. Plaster of paris, gesso, and acrylic polymer mediums, like Liquitex Modeling Paste or Liquitex Gel, are among the most popular. Any of these may be put on the board in generous amounts and spread, patted, or dabbed into a variety of textures and patterns. Modeling glues and the acrylic mediums, which may be used directly from the container, harden quickly. Plaster mixed with spackle dries more slowly, allowing time for experimentation (See Technical Notes, p. 68).

Color may be added to the modeling medium at any stage. Acrylic polymer paints come in a wide variety of colors that can be mixed with the Gel to produce any shade or hue. Color may be added to the plaster-spackle during the mixing process by adding powdered poster pigments or food coloring. Additional color effects may be developed by painting over the dried relief surface with oil paints, casein, or ordinary house paints.

Using mediums that can be modeled has an additional special advantage. Objects too stubborn to adhere with conventional glues may be set in place with the wet modeling medium. When the medium is dry, the stubborn object will be permanently affixed. This is particularly important when using heavy materials, such as metals, pieces of wood, or chunks of plastic.

69. In this collage, gesso was applied like heavy paint on a Masonite panel. (Covering Masonite with gesso has an advantage when working with tissues: the white gessoed surface allows the colors of the tissues to show to better advantage than does the dark brown of the Masonite.) After the gesso dried, Oriental papers and art tissues were laid over the surface. They were covered with a water-and-paste mixture, then worked into crinkles and folds to enhance the architectural quality of the collage.

70. Modeling mediums may be used to build up a surface relief. In this collage, charred newspapers, labels, and other printed papers were painted thoroughly with Liquitex medium, which dries transparent. The soaked papers were then placed on the board and worked into three-dimensional relief. Some of the areas were left fairly flat, while others were built into ridges and peaks.

71. Modeling paste was used here in an entirely different way to create texture and dimension. First, a thick coat of the medium was laid over a sturdy plywood panel. Then scraps of wood and metal, fabric strips, and veneer were placed in the viscous medium. When the medium had dried to the point where it was tacky to the touch, the objects were stripped off, leaving their textured imprints. The envelopes and advertisements were laid on when the medium was quite dry, and thin coats of colored Liquitex, oil, and casein were applied.

72. Here again an assortment of materials was laid on a piece of plywood coated with modeling paste. If you examine the center of the picture you can see that the "impressing" process was done more than once. The staff of the T shape and the deep lines below it were done first. Then pieces of veneer or fabric were pressed quickly into the almost dry medium.

APPLIED RELIEF

Any of a wide range of three-dimensional objects can be incorporated into a collage to create depth on the picture plane. Small items, like beans, soda bottle caps, washers and pebbles, may be used to create low relief effects, while larger objects, such as cigar boxes and wood fragments, will provide more dramatic contrasts.

Small, light items may be affixed with conventional glues. Large, heavy, or awkward materials will require steel glue or epoxy resins, or they may be imbedded in modeling mediums, as suggested in the previous section on built-up reliefs. The techniques presented

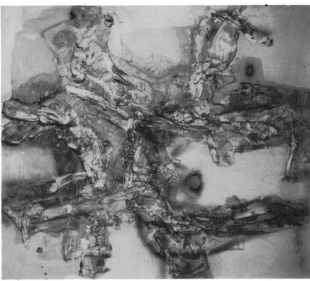

69. *ANCIENT ARCH by Mary Gehr*

70. *SCULPTURAL COLLAGE by Eve Garrison*

71. *SUNSET HOUSE by Gabriel Morera*
   Collection: Maureen Moran-Jones

72. *REPUBLICAN TICKET by Gabriel Morera*

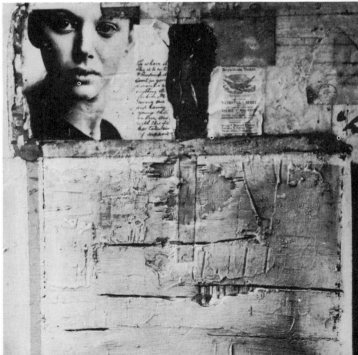

73. *ORCHARD by pre-school child*

74. *SPATIAL ABSTRACT by Eve Garrison, 1961*

in the following examples suggest several successful methods for adhering three-dimensional objects. They can be adapted to suit your own particular problems.

73. Almost anything can be used as applied dimension. This pre-schooler used felt, netting, cotton, buttons, cork, rice, broken egg shells, and paper. Children can be encouraged to divorce potential collage items from their familiar context by asking them of what else the item reminds them. One teacher went even further: She made each child choose his materials blind-folded. The child was then forced to find a new identification for each object.

74. A collage may employ both built-up and applied techniques. In this example, pieces of white carrara marble, ceramic tile, roofing tile, fabric, candy wrappers, and tin can covers were applied to a gessoed background.

75. Collage may also be used to create diorama-like pictures. Here the figures were cut from thin board and dressed, paper-doll style, in rich silks, furs, and other fancy fabrics, which were then pasted on. The scene was set in a box. The deliberate perspective of the three-dimensional table and archway adds to the feeling of depth. Most of the architectural details were cut and pasted.

75. *ST. JOHN NEPOMUCK CONFESSING THE QUEEN OF BOHEMIA*
by unknown artist, Southern Germany or Austria, c. 1750
Courtesy: The Cooper Union Museum, New York

76. *COLLAGE CONSTRUCTION by*
Robert W. Anderson, 1961

77. *FLOWERS OF GLASS AND GRASS*
by Ralph Arnold, 1961

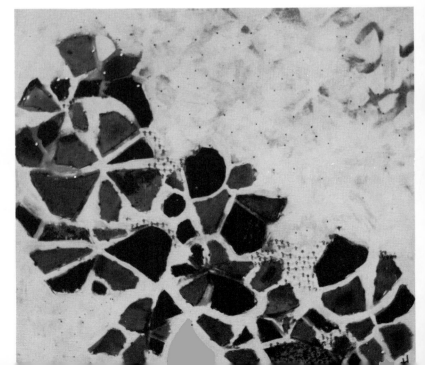

76. The edges and planes of three-dimensional objects reflect different amounts of light. This relief collage was designed to capitalize on this characteristic. The containers are placed so that their high lights and shadows are as integral to the composition as their shapes. Variation in light and dark has been planned within each closed area by using objects of different shapes and sizes. To create greater contrast, the background was painted with glossy white enamel.

77. Simplified petals of rusted tin and weathered glass have been glued and tacked on white pressed board. The board was then painted with gesso, into which sand and gravel were sifted for a rough textured effect.

78. Natural objects, gracefully arranged, make beautiful collages. However, glues and other conventional adherents are not too successful in holding them to the picture plane without damaging them. Japanese Teng-Jo paper, sometimes referred to as Sumi paper, solves this problem beautifully. Teng-Jo is a very soft, thin paper that partially disintegrates when a mixture of white glue and water is applied to its surface.

In the first illustration, the leaves are being arranged and held temporarily in place on the backing board with a dab of glue. After this placement, a dry sheet of Teng-Jo paper was placed over the arrangement. The second figure shows very thin watery glue being applied liberally to the paper. As the Teng-Jo disintegrates, the leaves will show through. The picture takes about twenty-four hours to set. All that remains of the Teng-Jo paper is the lacy, spidery traces of its threads, as seen in the finished illustration.

78. *COLEUS LEAVES by Dona Meilach, 1962*

6
Found Art

Found art refers to works of art composed of objects not normally thought of as art materials. Actually, most collages can be loosely thought of as found art. Many of the examples already discussed incorporate non-art materials. However, the term found art is usually restricted to the more three-dimensional constructions that are made up of items frankly known as junk.

Found art is a fascinating development of the contemporary art scene and one that arouses the curiosity of almost everyone. By developing works of art from found objects, the artist calls attention to the beauty of form and surface of everyday objects or items ready for the scrap heap. Considered separately, broken toys, worn-out can openers, pieces of wood, pencil sharpeners with missing parts and scraps of machinery no longer serve a useful purpose. They would certainly seem to have little to do with art. But in the hands of an adventurous artist, they can assume a new importance quite divorced from their original purpose.

The real mark of the developing creative mind is the visual pleasure it finds in all objects made by man. The artist, by removing the familiar thing from its accustomed niche and placing it in new surroundings and in unexpected,

ironic combinations, opens our eyes to the excitement and beauty in all forms. Children, who are less corrupted than adults in their evaluations of what is esthetically valid and what is not, take enormous pleasure in working imaginatively with found materials.

What makes junk items art media? What is done with them. They offer a ready-made and cheap source of unusual shapes, patterns, textures, and colors for the beginner and professional. It has been said that the greater the artist, the less prejudiced he is to humble things.

79. Weather-beaten wood, worn playing cards, and yellowed newspaper create a nostalgic recollection of the past. The small, rough-edged shapes seem to float over the solid larger forms, yet are visually connected by the horizontal and vertical orientation of all the found objects.

80. Onto a round wood base, pieces of driftwood are interspersed with "man-shaped" wood segments and fragments of a shattered mannequin head. The result is an undulating, jagged mass which breaks the bounds of the surface plane. The composition utilizes the natural differences in tone of the found objects to build up a dark focal area that counterbalances the simple arrangement of light segments.

79. *UNTITLED CONSTRUCTION by Ralph Arnold*

80. *LA SOMNAMBULE* by Don Baum, 1962

81. *THE TICKLER by Don Baum, 1962*
photo by Aaron Siskind

82. *A PONY RIDE by Don Baum, 1962*
photo by Aaron Siskind

81. Weathered wood, worn brushes, broken handles, and rubber tubing comprise this highly textured construction. A formal, quasi-geometric arrangement is achieved both by the artist's careful organization and by the very nature of the objects used.

82. A long oval is the basis for this assemblage of driftwood, work boards, paper, and pieces of a child's plastic horse.

83. A strong tactile feeling is achieved by contrasting natural wood and sand with a painted plywood mounting. The objects are affixed with polyester resin.

84. Found objects are assembled to create a three-dimensional symbol of the carousel. The materials are paper, wood, mirrors, and wire netting.

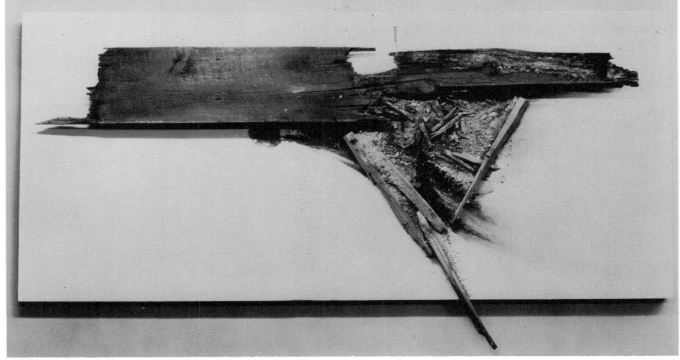

83. *IN FLIGHT by Robert Mallary*
    Collection: Museum of Modern Art,
    New York, Larry Aldrich Foundation Fund

84. *CENTRAL PARK CAROUSEL by*
    Joseph Cornell. Collection: Museum
    of Modern Art, New York, The
    Katherine Cornell Fund

85. *LESSER SOURCE by Harry Bouras, 1962*

86. *BROOM BIRD by Tomi Ungerer*
Courtesy: D'Arcy Galleries, New York

85. This is a good example of using man-made materials to interpret an occurrence in nature. A seed's growth into a plant, as seen from deep within the earth, has been developed through the use of welded sheet metal and rods. The solid nature of the earth is represented by the concrete in which the metal is embedded. A living quality is suggested by the interplay of light and shadow.

86, 87, 88. Art is certainly where you find it. In this case, the source was the trash can. The humorous possibilities of found art assemblages are delightfully realized in these animals, put together from an odd assortment of abandoned and defunct items.

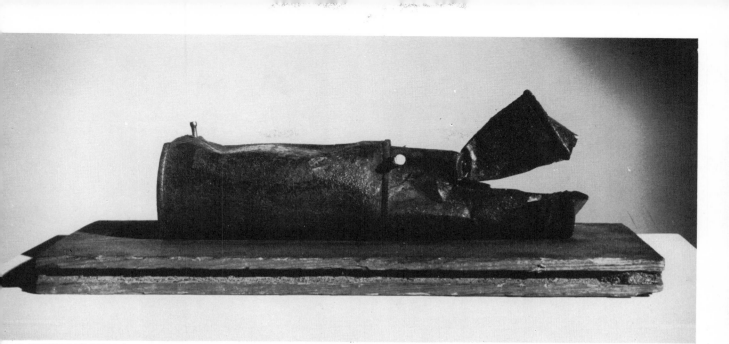

37. LAUGHING HIPPO by Tomi Ungerer. Courtesy: D'Arcy Galleries, New York

38. RAT by Tomi Ungerer. Courtesy: D'Arcy Galleries, New York

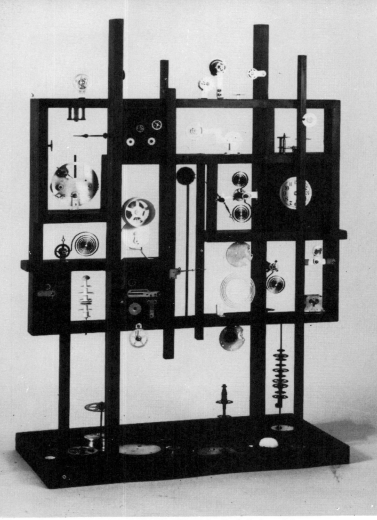

89. *CONSTRUCTION TO TIME by Ralph Arnold, 1961*

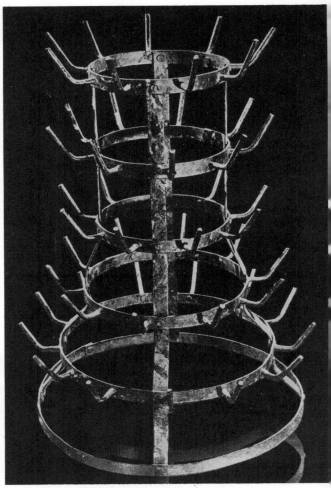

90. *BOTTLE NECK by Marcel Duchamp*
Collection: Museum of Modern Art, New York

89. This fully three-dimensional assemblage is made of wood and mechanisms from antique clocks. The wood was used to construct open rectangles that frame the intricate metallic forms. Many of the clockworks are mounted so that they move and quiver with the slightest motion. A scale model was made first, then projected into the final construction.

90. Relieved of its commonplace function, this metal rack for drying bottles assumes a striking resemblance to contemporary sculpture.

91. Commonplace things when seen through the eyes of the artist assume an almost haunting personality. The artist-photographer who recorded these images encourages us to enjoy the colors, shapes, and textures found in objects that we see every day. This is found art in its purest state, and is as compelling in its way as the works assembled by the artist.

91. *FOUND OBJECTS* photographed by Ivan Chermayeff

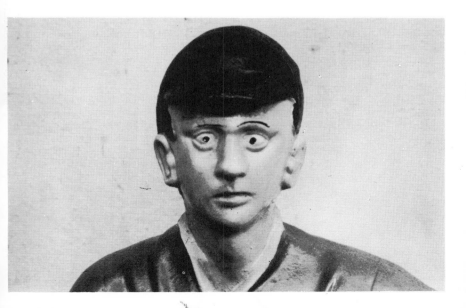

Acknowledgments

The preparation of this book has been a heartwarming experience, thanks to the many people who contributed ideas and examples of their work. To the many artists who contributed their works our sincerest thanks.

We appreciate the cooperation of the Art Institute of Chicago; Findlay Galleries, Chicago; Cooper Union Museum, the Museum of Modern Art, and the D'Arcy Galleries in New York, who made reproductions of works in their collections available to us.

To the schools and art teachers who made student work available, we are particularly grateful: Richard Brouillette, Art Director, Evergreen Park Community High School, Evergreen Park, Illinois; Miss Joan Ferstenberg, Art Specialist, Bellmore Elementary Schools, Bellmore, Long Island; Beth Torah Religious School; Faulkner School for Girls, Chicago; Mrs. Thyra Ryan, O'Connor Day Nursery, Beverly, Illinois; Harold Stevens, Garden School, New York; and Dr. N. I. Krevitsky, Art Supervisor, Tucson Public School. And our special thanks to the students themselves.

For photographic advice we are indebted to Norman Maks, Virginia Gedney, Allen Meilach, and Jim Taylor.

Technical Notes

The main body of the text is concerned with developing aesthetic awareness through collage. The book was not meant to be a technical manual. However, some technical information is necessary, and so the following basic information is presented as a brief guide.

ORIENTAL PAPERS

Oriental papers come in a wide variety of textures and colors. The most popular and versatile include:

Kinwashi—Very soft with overall texture. White, blue, green, orange.

Cloud Paper—Beige and blue silk threads embedded in fine thin white paper.

Unryu—Very soft white with yellow silk threads throughout.

Tobi Kumo—Light brown with circular texture of dark browns that resemble curls of hair.

Krinkle—Raised surface textured paper in many colors.

Lace Paper—Sheer, web-like cutouts in several patterns. Pastel shades.

Batik—Beige and brown textured.

Sugi Kawa—Rough dark brown with beige and brown flecks.

Shoji—All over textured paper in a variety of colors.

Mingei—Solid colors like construction paper but softer and more pliable. May be used wet.

Origami—Solid and patterned. Colors run when wet.

Tea Chest—Solid gold and silver. Also gold and silver with prints.

Sakura—Soft paper with printed designs.

Teng-Jo—Very thin, almost transparent.

MAKING CORRECTIONS

Occasionally a shape or object won't look right after it has been pasted down. To remove an undesirable paper shape, wet a small sponge and lay it over the shape. In a few seconds, the water will have soaked down through the paper to the paste and the paste will soften. Simply lift the shape and pat away remaining paste with a damp sponge.

If you have pasted down a large or bulky object, apply a wet sponge around the edges. Lift the object gradually, applying the sponge to the still adhered areas.

PLASTER-SPACKLE MIXTURE

Plaster of paris and powdered spackle may be obtained from a hardware or paint supply store or a building materials outlet. Plaster is quite cheap by the pound. Spackle is slightly more expensive.

For mixing you will need either a clean half-gallon milk carton with the top cut off or a flexible-plastic (polyethylene) bowl. When through with the carton, you can simply throw it away. If the mixture dries and cakes in the plastic bowl, twist the bowl out of shape and the plaster-spackle will shatter and flake. It can then be easily picked out, and the bowl is ready for re-use. Warning: Do not throw plaster or spackle down drains; it will clog them.

To make your medium, pour water into the container; do not put the dry ingredients in first. The amount of water needed depends upon your specific requirements, but remember that it is better to have too much medium than too little. Into the water, sprinkle the plaster and spackle until they form a slight peak above the water line. The ratio of plaster to spackle depends upon how much time you need to work. The more time, the more spackle. A 1:1 ratio will allow about 20 minutes working time before the mixture hardens. After the peak is formed, stir the mixture with a spoon or stick until it is creamy and has no lumps. Do not stir with your fingers; plaster is very irritating to the skin. At this point you may add poster paints or food coloring, if you wish. When the mixture is thoroughly stirred, it is ready for use.